"The poems in *Learned* feel like an underbelly, and they feel like the knife tip, and they feel like the cut—a chorus of identities, held precariously in one fierce speaker coming undone and becoming something new. Carellin Brooks' poetry is the raw, chaotic interior of a heart pouring out through a speaker who invites you under her skin just to understand what she is. Vulnerable and determined, *Learned* is an invitation you won't want to turn down, for a journey that will never leave you."
—Nic Brewer, author of *Suture*

———•———

"An exuberant Blakean song—of experience and innocence, of body and mind. With wry wit, Brooks evokes a unique education—Oxford by day, London by night—and hard-won enlightenment."
—Brett Josef Grubisic, author of *My Two-Faced Luck*

———•———

"Brooks writes with clear forward-looking eyes about how she reclaimed her command of her body after sexual violation and abuse. Her lines are chiselled, ragged and disorienting, evoking the intensity of her transformation as she plays with the limits of bearable pain, which overlap here with the bounds of memory. The balm of this book is Brooks makes no attempt to put her learning in a box, or to label it as knowledge—the learning is there for us lucky readers to turn over, inspect, and glean the dark glimmers and glorious bruises of her story."
—Alex Leslie, author of *Vancouver for Beginners* and *We All Need to Eat*

"Part dream or fantasy, part role play, these are half-remembered poems from a disappearing life, a hushed ego trying to recall its origins. They function like a hole in a public stall, a peep show, allowing only glimpses of the speaker's sexual education. She records her younger self navigating that illicit grey zone between pleasure and pain, permission and complicity, and control as a tool for release, perhaps to remake how she understands the history of her body, and what others have done and can now do with it. Playful, sometimes frightening, always beguiling poems, from a writer I greatly admire."

—Michael V. Smith, author of *Bad Ideas*

"The miracle of the novel is that Brooks never runs out of original and startling ways to describe precipitation. The consistently riveting and beautiful descriptions of weather stand as testament to Brooks' rare talent."
—*Quill & Quire*

"A truly snackable book... set in Vancouver, rain's epicentre, and the author uses the many forms of daily precipitation to mirror her deftly wrought tale of stress, heartache and rebirth."
—*Toronto Star*

"That the world comes down on us if we make art of it or not is true. Rain as the agent of how much is beyond our control, thus this book opens into such questions as how to fully inhabit both loss and beauty and how to let the natural world save you. Brooks doesn't profess; she asks and observes."
—*Lambda Literary Review*

Book*hug Press
Toronto 2022

Learned

POEMS

CARELLIN BROOKS

FIRST EDITION
© 2022 by Carellin Brooks

Library and Archives Canada Cataloguing in Publication

Title: Learned / Carellin Brooks.
Names: Brooks, Carellin, author.
Description: Poems.
Identifiers: Canadiana (print) 20220210063 | Canadiana (ebook) 20220210071
   ISBN 9781771667876 (softcover)
   ISBN 9781771667883 (EPUB)
   ISBN 9781771667890 (PDF)
Classification: LCC PS8603.R6593 L43 2022 | DDC C811/.6—dc23

The production of this book was made possible through the generous assistance of the Canada Council for the Arts and the Ontario Arts Council. Book*hug Press also acknowledges the support of the Government of Canada through the Canada Book Fund and the Government of Ontario through the Ontario Book Publishing Tax Credit and the Ontario Book Fund.

Book*hug Press acknowledges that the land on which we operate is the traditional territory of many nations, including the Mississaugas of the Credit, the Anishnabeg, the Chippewa, the Haudenosaunee, and the Wendat peoples. We recognize the enduring presence of many diverse First Nations, Inuit, and Métis peoples and are grateful for the opportunity to meet, work, and learn on this territory.

Book*hug Press

To all my teachers
past and present

Contents

Fixed

* * *

(First Media Interview, Montreal, Spring 1993)

Photographer first. Posed in apartment's empty parlour:
daylight-flooded eyes fixed on invisible future.
Embossed wallpaper, jade plant, platinum crop.
Look at me: all picture, all surface, all gloss.

Roommate rattling pots. *When will he be done, eh.*

Black leather biker jacket shrugged over,
thick hide, weight of comfort. *Protect me.*

From what though? I'd won.
The reward for the years bent to the desk.
Handed in on time every assignment.
Start anew, life of the mind, concentrated. Essential.

Reporter on the phone: *But what about you?*
Our readers want to know: How did you learn?
Richest scholarship in the Western world. Anywhere, really.
Funded by diamonds, wasn't it?
Tainted blood, cut facet.
Ruthless exploitation. How can you justify—

Did you really grow up in foster care?
Could you just explain,
abandoned by both parents in turn by the age of—

So young. Surely nobody would ever
accuse you of doing anything wrong,
to provoke such a catastrophe.

Then consigned, I understand,
*to a man who took—*cleared his throat
How did you, um, recover?

Most with your background don't finish high school, much less
make it to university, much less graduate and then win
such a prestigious worldwide award. Wouldn't you agree?

Can you explain why you turned out
different? Would you say your
orientation, as you people call it,
was caused by your
history of abuse?

*Or perhaps you see yourself as a role model?**

---

* Picked nose, scratched scabs,
  blackheads *hardly* the thing, academic life.
  Make myself a vessel, empty and bleached.
  Purity. *Higher things.*

Where do you see yourself in five, ten years?
Political leader? Captain of industry?

How do you feel? Have you dreamed of this for years
the way a girl dreams
of her wedding day?

You must be smart.

═══

Never learned French,
maudite anglais—
shrink from world outside.

Absent for the Grade 5
menstruation talk (got the pamphlet
but never caught up,
apparently still
a mystery this body of mine
powers of attraction despite my will and best efforts,
bit of a disaster so far really)

No contest.

Slip

(Montréal, Spring 1993, New York, Summer 1993,
B.C., Summer 1978, Summer 1981)

A grey man calls, a mathematician.
Head of the scholarship committee.

Handhold sweaty grip plastic telephone receiver.
Sudden bloom of underarm sweat.
Asserted body, troublesome as ever.
Stomach drop, buzz in chest. *Help me.*

Just one vote to seal my fate
(didn't say).

Will he unbend?
Ridiculous. Confess:
I've never known what to do.

Now less than ever
at this supposed moment of triumph.
You see I'm untethered
Nobody to turn to not even
the woman who asks me for only one thing—simple
uncomplicated *Give me* and I sink willingly
gladly even.

See parents had a habit of slipping

out of one's grasp—fingers stretch—
mother lost. Didn't die.
Left (age eight) father followed (eleven)
foster family step in take over stay
foster father had his way well enough
about that but the body always remembers, doesn't it?
For good or ill the body keeps its dumb faith.

Hands and pleadings my turn to slip finally but:
carry with me still the

new knowledge
inadvertent betrayal
terrible consequence
for such unremarkable flesh:
fat gather small breasts chicken thigh.

Confess: no
plan no grand ambitions no scheme
for advancement survive that's all.

But then: books.
Block out the world
or at least have all the answers,
everything solved by the end.
All clear
close covers
shut eyes
no whispers
sleep easy
never have to hear

Let me
I know
you want
it

Arrow to teacher's straight lines
due date exclamation: *Excellent!*
Always with that mark.
Here I belong. Right?

Pull up relocate body gone astray
wandered long ago. Pawned
shiny coin
lost value.
Redeem myself.

Wonderland

* * *

(Oxford, Michaelmas 1993)

Green lawns, champagne flutes aloft,
fluttered white dresses. *1936.*
Of course these days it's no picnic—
Firsts, tutorials, chambered rooms, open fires,
dons in gowns leaning forward breathless.
Could I interest you, sherry and port.
Blinking behind glasses at my unsuspected brilliance.
Ah yes. You put it very well indeed.
Then the same mark on the paper: *Excellent!*

First morning grey
like all those to come,
sleepless lined faces,
crumpled coats under slate sky,
queue (here to learn),

eyes glued sandy.
Bus pull up, snort and sigh,
an hour, two, three,
then lurch let out at the college gates.

Smooth stone walls
stretched up to same-coloured sky.
Cutouts at the top, castle-like. Crenellations.
Boiling oil for the barbarian hordes. *Not us.*

Welcome. Go Away.
Enormous door, land locked.
Timbers girded with iron. Tiny door's reluctant admittance.
I stepped inside, over the bowed threshold.
Consented, as in all the grimmest fairy tales.
A man waited as if for me alone. Glass box, exhibit A.
The first representative of this august assemblage.
Keeper at the gate, grossly pink. *Yes?*

Cleared my throat.* Announced my name.
No surprise, apparently. Slid open, drawn out
key from a worn slot.
Follow the path.

---

* Red tongue behind
  tight lips. Licked.
  Turned a smudged page, flutter,
  sinking newsprint
  smile. Flat double nipple,
  sprawling punch line under thick fingers.

Pallid turquoise case, vinyl sides, wrist loop.
Rolled lawns,** stone flags, shadowed arches, shut buttery,
steps bowed in the middle, seven hundred years' worth, up and
    down again.
Wooden benches, paned windows with raised eyebrows looking
    over.
Just like I'd imagined, only more so. The grounds, the keep, our
    splendid—
All this just for me?

Tugged my case, went back.
My 64K word processor. Timid query,
inconvenient physicality, *refreshment,* out of place. *Excuse me—*

A shrug. *No.*

Silent hall. Dank open corridor. Fitful light.
Then a courtyard: two diminutive houses facing each other.
A set of steps for me to mount. Locked door.
Inside: chair, desk, a bed,
a bare mattress.
Striped pillow,
ticking,
leaking tiny feathers

**Not supposed to walk on them,
    I'd gathered,
    though not why.

Alice

* * *

(Oxford, Michaelmas 1993, New York, Summer 1993)

Tired punch-drunk
sleep fled from planes or buses
all the little bottles *drink me*

Try to forget. Vain instruction as ever.
How to obliterate Mick's (1993)
hand on shoulder
pressing down, mouth open *Yes?*
Knees ground into cheap motel room carpet
You like this don't you?
Yes. But she's gone now,
like everyone else. Or me.
No more of that now.

No anaesthesia turns out
for that sweet torn memory.
Flight arrested, dropped like a shot bird, through thick cloud.
Debarked in disarray, dishevelled.
Anyway I'll never have to—

Thrust my hand in the box.
Smooth sheet of white paper
quarterly amounts, pounds sterling, dull coins
weight warmed metal dropping in my palm
ransom bride's price forfeit.

No front door coconut matting *Welcome (Go Away)*
Chopped in rough
miniature rectangle, hobbit's
fairy tale entrance.
It's fine, I've been lots of places
Not like this where I didn't fit in at first,
where everyone stared in silence
spine tingle crawling scalp
Perfectly all right
Just fine

Yes? He already knows.
Confession? Just like all the
places I've arrived with what
I could drag in two hands bowed
seven hundred years' stone steps
bowed in the middle
by the feet of every other student passing through.
Seize my box, lift it into the air: almost weightless.

Anyplace to get something to eat?
Ask, beg, demand.
Open my empty mouth.
Silent hall, dank open corridor, fitful light
invisible ink nonetheless
marking me as
impermanent.
Skeleton key fumble, fit, and turn.
No case, no sheets, no cover.
Stuffing hand
to mouth
one sob.
So tired.

Moral Tutor

* * *

(Oxford, Michaelmas Term 1993)

Crossed the High. Miniature van *beep beep*
approaching at speed from the left (nearly hit).
Breathless instructions: *Dear Barber, leave two spots. One above*
each temple. Otherwise pare
my hair to the skull.
I'd wax the spots as they grew. Horns.
Posed for a library card.
White collar and a little black dress. Smiled
for the picture. Swore an oath.
Promise not to set fire to any books.

A card in my box, college's name impressed on top. Small caps.
  Do drop in—
Moral Tutor. Up stone stairs, following the porter's—
*But what? Who's—*Shut up. Knock knock.
Father, may I?

Penned up paper thin
stacked flat all life long. Sandy hair and sketch face.
No register. Blue eyes maybe. Dry sticklike figure
creased at the torso like wet card,
under a skim-milk shirt.

He offered coffee. *Oh thanks. So kind—*
Instant granules spooned into a mug.
Spoon hovered. *Creamer?*
Chipped from a jar.

Ignored/didn't notice my surprised *Oh.*

So you've a scholarship then? Ah yes. Some of them do qualify
Paused, sucked, gob stopper let out
eventually.

Flushed. First test. *Don't mind.*
Passed over the insipid brew.
Untasted cup, dissolved essence ignored edge of desk.
Leaned closer so eager was I to kindle—*My vision.*
Keen to read about write about women.
Dilated: *Characters, sex,*
how they discover themselves that way.
The acquisition of knowledge.
The bildungsroman, *yes,*
but a sexual one.

I think it's entirely relevant—Marvelled. Listen to myself
sounding learned. Waited for him to recognize our shared
   desire:
safely slipped in between flat white sheets.

Sounds like you are unequipped, he went,
*for the life academic. Many
have tried. A failed project
ultimately, in the main.
By all means though, do give it a go.*
He stood, dismissing me.
I should of course wish you luck. *
No doubt you can succeed here, he smiled,
should you devote your scholarship
cough
Regrettably so often you Americans—
But, I sputtered, rose in my turn—
murmured
fundamentally lacking

* —not glancing at my white-collared dress
or the furred spots on my skull.
So I had to go then, didn't I, leave book-lined
familiar surroundings Exhibit A
mute and betraying flesh
continuing mystery
sealed until now, Pandora's
give it a crack
all she needs

Dungeon 101

* * *

(London, Winter 1993)

London calling. Mid-sixties modern university. Floating stairs
cantilever.
Neophyte, *ingenue*, first-timer *I can* here to learn *maybe* I
forced to the floor *don't* breathe.

Looky-loo. Men in leather,
women in ponytails wearing bridles
buckled cuffs stitched leather straps stainless rings
buttless chaps plaid shirts sliding gaze
little deviltry.

Upstairs, willing victim long-laddered back
expressionless young man, sandy hair and sketch face
demonstrating each sensation:
When applying pressure, maintain a constant tension.

He tugs the clamps and her gasp ripples across us watching.
Keep in mind that bruises—smack—
will not appear for some time.
Blood in the urine is a danger sign.
Blond, mildly enquiring, studied
neutrality. Guide to our particular ethics.
Seek immediate medical attention. Follow our protocols.
Arrange concealment of wounds and bruising,
if without a car take a taxi if funds allow,
tell hospital personnel as little as possible.
Men especially will be held on suspicion of abuse
if you try to explain.
Get out as quick as you can, carry your partner
if she cannot walk, call
a friend. Please.

Right then. Anyone else
like to give it a go?

Must move, say something,
open my empty mouth—
silent the crowd rumbles good nature
can smell their concentration salty and hot
first cut wipes everything else clean,
clear skies no fear.

Pain's utility.
Beckon, the always
available friend,
Yoo hoo, guaranteed relief.

First bit of kit: spanking-new chest harness,
stiff strapped bobbing breasts
perked up by their odd situation
Fancy seeing you here

rubber straps constricting breath.
Invite myself along for drinks,
ignoring the human pony's marked
lack of enthusiasm. Another queue then inside
chain link–scored sheet metal walls,
lean, wave vainly to the bartender— *Yoo hoo*—
then a voice
from another world (mine)

blond quiff, Roman nose:
not girlfriend material but
could guide me in this
new world

turned
hurled myself
You're Canadian

Plucked, held at arm's length,
two breasts impassively examined
You too

Heard & Said

$*\ \ *\ \ *$

(The Vault, London, Winter 1993)

Hi, good to meet you I said *My name is*
just got here, lots of ideas ready
to start exploring, do you like my harness, cool isn't it,
you should see all the—

> *Let's get a few things clear right from the start,*
> *wouldn't want to give you*
> *the wrong impression.*
> *If you're into that kind of stuff*
> *I have little to say to you.*

I've had to, well, flee isn't quite the word,
I had a difficult time, had to grow up, like they say,
fast, when I—Anyway
I barely know you after all, so let me, um, change the subject, talk
    about my—

      That's quite the impressive package,
      prestigious scholarship, so well endowed.
      What research are you planning again?

I have this idea, it sounds kind of stupid when I
say it out loud, I'm, like, discovering myself—

      I've met your kind before, think you
      know everything, led a sheltered life,
      oh I'm sure I'll hear all about
      your so-called disadvantaged background—

      I've met your type before,
      this discovery you're after,
      down some girl's pants no doubt

this is a fabulous opportunity (for me)

      You come over here without a thought
      beyond what's in it for you,
      not that you notice much past your swollen egos,
      no care for the locals you leave
      behind when you blithely wave goodbye.
      Why do I care, well I'm from
      Canada too but I live here see
      and have to mop up the messes you leave behind

Well since you ask, a guy hit me, no,
not like that, a demonstration, how to
flog someone safely, I'm telling you
the very first blow had no idea,
my own body returned to me (with interest), *
you know those dreams
where you recognize the place but when you wake up
you realize you've never been there before?

Like coming home

> *No*
> *rules, is that it?** You think you can just leave?*
> *Not spare a thought for whatever you discard on the way*
> *out?*
> *You think pain is something you can play with*
> *and feeling is something you can leave behind*
> *with your stupid safe words, yes I know a bit about it,*
> *nothing convinces me it's anything but self-indulgent*
> *foolishness*
> *and let's pretend for people who are supposedly old enough to*
> *know better.*
> *But you're a nice girl no doubt despite your attention-seeking*
> *outfits*
> *now put on a coat*

---

*Remembering New York in the summertime, Mick
thought it was just her.
Never felt that way until her hand in me.

** Wave at the bartender like a prat, complain about the food
like you're the first person ever—
Fuck the locals.

Will you walk me to my bus? Yes, Oxford. I go to Victoria.
Every twenty minutes, escape route, ha ha. I love
your nose. So what do you do? A chef? Oh that's interesting, oh it*
isn't? Walk with me. It's so cold. Look at
me.

*Can't say that.

On Offer

* * *

(King's Cross, Autumn 1993)

What would you get up to if left to your own devices.
No point arguing. Sigh. I'll just have to come with you.

Tube to anonymous nondescript streets
stacked brick buildings, humped indistinct masses
open doorway, blank warehouse front, dim bulb.
Spiky-haired fish-netted girl
folding table perch, enamelled cash box
black lipstick, lidded weight, silver-scaled glance
taking in Canadian's khaki trousers
No fetishwear? Extra twenty quid then.

Inside the cavernous dark cathedral heights
stern mistress stalks by, gaze fixed on invisible future
leashed slave on all fours scrambling to follow
Lucky I murmur inaudible, face aflame, averted
metallic taste bump gritted teeth
horse's bit, metal chew, sucked smooth.
Could I, is that what I want?

Each niche around the circumference of the vast space
a separate saint's sanctum.
Holy wax dripped on writhing form,
acolytes bending to the rack. Drawn-out howl.
Noooo. Squirming
in sympathy and?

Continue the tour.
Merchandise area another gauntlet to run
Care to try our new electrical device?
Twiddling the knobs
Some people find it quite...stimulating!

Make-believe, fairy tales, dress-up for adults.
Ooh I'm so scared.
The Canadian waves.
What's the point?

Don't you want to be someone else?
More exciting? (Sideways at her Dockers)
Braver? (Cheap sex-shop vinyl mini)
Dangerous? (Faraway blows, grunts)
An enormous man in hip waders
salty and hot smell of him
catches sight of me sniffing nasal *Yes?*

Don't you ever want to disappear?

Orange Crush

* * *

(Oxford, Michaelmas Term 1993, B.C., Summer 1978)

Settled down in.
Charity shops' stacked sheets
soft from washing, felt-tipped name of previous owner
bleeding black into hems.
Creased volunteer rang me up where I stood
clutching my thick bundle.
Used plastic carrier bag crinkled already.
Pound coin, *thunk*, till.
There you are, luv.

Account at the bank. Manager's hand rub:
Yes, certainly.
Assets to set against my losses.
Trail of lefts
stretched all the way back

to my mother, slipped away
when I was eight—
That won't happen again,
you're the anointed one now, see.
Saw it all
over: late-afternoon sunlight,
car drawn up running, reedy child's voice
Where do I go?
Leaned out. Mop of red hair, crisp instruction.
Try your father.
Raised cloud of dust obscure and squint after away.

Suddenly single no longer.*
Planning meeting, the campus gay group
looking for next year's executive.
Plastic beakers, inky tipple.
Top you up?
Taught me the designation for unfortunates like her: *ginger*,
all-night shop: *garage*, and tampons: *Lillets*.
A whole new language. Finished
bottle of claret in a paper twist, slurred
What are you like then?

Raised a toast
shoulder to shoulder, narrow single bed.
Crumpled jeans and sheets. More new phrases:
Non-starter,
big girl's blouse

---

*Ginger crewcut girlfriend, guide (1993–94)
red flake–sprinkled skin. Man behind the bar
always taking her for a child: *Sorry, sonny,*
you have to be twelve to play the fruit machine.
Told the story to all her mates and me laughing
Hilarious I tried.

Ginger Snap

* * *

(Oxford, Michaelmas Term 1993, B.C., Summer 1978)

How are you faring then.
Have you a battels card for the buttery yet.
Did you get your stipend.

Tell the Moral Tutor my plan
to investigate sexual knowing—*Yes of course.*
Hand flap quick dismissal. Doesn't want to know.

But—empty corridor, closed door,
hand wrung, still wondering.

Suppose I've done everything wrong so far?
Supposed to know just like
supposed to know before.

It's your father's turn.
My mother's edict, car idling in the driveway.
Afterwards, only one
guilty party:
why didn't I see this coming?

Meet the Canadian down the pub.
Cut off my rendition of my latest exploits—*Listen.*
Do me a favour, would you? Stick to other expats maybe?
Not me, a shudder, *some hope, but surely there's*

Nonsense. Put it into words.
Me and Ginger settled all that. It's sorted, I try.
Ginger isn't looking for anything else, anything
long-term.
So you're planning on seeing other people?
What about her?
The locals don't get the concept of non-monogamy.
We're talking different languages.
Elide the question instead. Repeat:
Of course she knows

Beats Me

* * *

(Venus Rising, Brixton, 1994)

Crowded house
before the club *Something Arms*
got drunk on pints, piss-poor
lager watered
cider tang froth of
white bride's lace
sink purple snake's bite
She'll have a Blackbeard,
shaven pate crowded in next.
Saw you at the S&M conference.
All yap. Bloody foreigner.
Shut your gob, drink that.
Proffered hand. *Pearl.*
Delicious

Pearl* nodded satisfied.
Thought you'd. Guinness and Coke.

Locals hunched over like pints of poor
piss gold. Teen barmaids,
pink-cheeked, braved
leather-jacketed baying crowd,
invincible indifference
I think I know what to do,
I shouted to Pearl.
We stood on club
catwalk, metal mesh

*Lecturer in textiles at the university.
Hand-sewn corset her graduate project,
bleached muslin, each rib
encased in a
form-fitting sheath,
careful stitching.

Pearl's teeth blue-framed like old tile
what a surprise knobby skull something of the moors,
to her standing as in the full brunt of the wind.

Girlfriend named Weldon, slab-like.
Wore always a leather biker jacket,
stainless cock ring threaded through left-hand epaulet.
Black hanky. *Shocker.*
Pearl and Weldon went to Wales.
Driving holiday. *What did you do?*
Heard a cry,
stopped and rescued a lamb
that had gotten stuck.

underfoot, wink and blinding flash
of revolving spots. Women bobbing in white vests below.
Blue glow of their torsos twisting
toward us then away.
I think I'll write about
women's sexuality. I think I can
make a case for what they learn.

Pearl cupped an ear.
What? I can't hear you.

The music faded.
A second's silence.

Oh, here Pearl turned
Meet my flatmate. **

**David Bowie circa 1975.
Jacket with exaggerated shoulder pads
zippered diagonally hip to shoulder.

Bones sticking out, only a thin covering
of skin to hold them in, like Frankenstein's monster
(good way).

Learned later: motorbike courier,
had an accident,
couldn't drive anymore.
Actually had driven
a moped.

Randy

* * *

(Hackney, 1994)

How about a walk,
Randy declares.
No dinner, no drinks, no movie? *OK.*
The park innocuous, yellow and brown,
last of winter's sodden squish underfoot.

Trips,
holds me down. *Hey.*
Her face above mine, blue sky behind craggy, deeply lined.
Rummages in my clothes, tumbled white spear first shoots veg cart

barrow boy, marrow and rocket,
brown paper bag, twisted present. *There you are, luv.*
Work-roughened hands, no false nicety—*OK?*

Known quantity, arrows to the line
splitting the middle. Pierces my
ordinary patter—
Ah. Two Labrador retrievers sniffing over,
bed of wet dead leaves pressed underneath.
Faraway walkers. Faraway path. Randy kneeling, hands full
Get off
and from even farther away
the shout of their names.
How I laugh. Randy stands, dusts her clothes.
Two wet patches, either knee, punctuate
narrow trousers, stovepipe legs.
Come on. Puts out a hand. Hauls me up.

Pearl next morning,
hip cocked between me and the
coffee maker. Draws her robe tight—

*Didn't you say you
got a scholarship in your country?*

Uh-huh.
Reach past her for the pot. No joy.

So you can't, she continues,
really be that stupid.

Can you?

Lesson Plan

* * *

(Bodleian Library, Oxford, Hilary Term 1994)

Look. Plato's behind Socrates
proffering the card.

It's reversed, get it?
Eager explanation, too intent.
Told myself *stop talking* but I couldn't.
Plato is the pupil, see, but he's the one behind, like he's actually
penetrating the master, the teacher,
the one who imparts knowledge.
There's a whole book of theory about it.
And you can still buy the postcard right here—
Standing in the gift shop.

Hm robin's egg blue'd glance briefly alighting then
flicked again to invisible future

Call f'you, porter had wheezed. Feeble flap of beefy hand
too enervated to point. Newspaper held fast, pinned by thick
   flesh.
Page-three grainy reproduction peeking out under his fingers.
Two breasts, sunny side up, model smile.

Plastic receiver clutch
sudden slip of greased palm
like yesterday
my mother's voice down the telephone line.

How did you find me? Still that same reedy
Told myself *Stop it. Not a child anymore.*
Stood, listened: pulse thrum throat flutter constrict.

Oh, Hamish and I are touring Hadrian's wall.
First I'd heard.
*We have a tower in our house, circular. I want
to turn it into a library.*
Can you show me?

Sure, swallowed, ignored blood's leap for release, skin flush.
Um, Duke Humfrey's, it's where they keep the pornography.
Letter pi, mimeographed sheets
hand-lettered thermal paper slip and purple curl
Can you believe?

Knowing already
I'd lose. Too much too felt too urgent
unanswered questions. She'd never say
everything I needed to know.
Even if she did, still wouldn't explain.

Watched her leave. Habit, familiar now.
Still echoed that first rending and deep toothache:
frizz of red hair rising above the collar,
military-cut coat, epaulets marshalling each shoulder.
Buttons in a double row down the front. Quicksilver.
Same walk, same haste, rush to next
nothing important crucial *Now*.

But what about you?
Ginger girlfriend arrived breathless,
apologies flurried
In the lab experiment
crucial stage sorry couldn't.

Too late to meet my mother, explain *I'm her—*
Didn't she want to know? How it's going? Anything?

She's not like that, I said.

What, human?

First Try (Dark Blues)

* * *

(Cherwell River, Oxford, Trinity Term 1994)

Punt
gliding under low branches
we duck,
wondered glance, watery sunshine,
nodding daffs, budded trees,
third term: we've survived.
Plastic glasses, Pimm's
bump, all a-jostle:
floating fruit slice, citrus oil.
Sharp gooey bloom. I rise,
grasp the pole surprised,
sucking river muddy bottom.
Clutch and reluctant release
our speared connection,
world above, sky, surface flutter.

Stuck in. Cherwell. Isis.
Uh-huh. Starved
for mother, show her, pass,
scooped white dress. Architecture
of bone limned in bleached cotton
soft less

The Parks, choir May Day morn, the balls
(not me; too expensive by half)
broken only by first light,
dishevelled undergraduates
staggering home
still in evening dress, broken beading,
commoners' gowns, bare feet,
straps in hand.
Bicycles thrown into the river
at term's end, wheel rims breaking the surface
of the lowered, levelled stream.

Corner shops' serried ranks
of postcards, Oxford gargoyles
fixed in air,
invisible above our daily passages.
Stone faces deeply scored
with torment and despair,
mouths gaping. Anguished cries.
Half-written dispatches.
Our already voided lament—richest scholarship
scaled pinnacle, career made:
can't wait to come home,
been cold now
for eight months.
No way to explain, no place to add our postscript
shivering under
thin blankets,

drifting downriver

lost

A Cup

* * *

(Oxford to Soho, Long Vac 1994)

London calling. Down or up again.
Napped bus seat, bristles
brushing backs of bare thighs,
sun shifting in window.
Joined thighs' sticky clasp,
skin to skin, pull suck.

Impromptu
alfresco airing, Hyde Park.
Winter white two bared
breasts bits and bobs
weeping willow imperfect concealment
turned out. Outraged gamekeeper,
thick Scottish accent, had to repeat himself three times
before I understood:

threatened my arrest
on grounds of indecent exposure.

New demographic, market to us.
Bus ads—tongued models, gamine short cuts,
pallid pierced spaghetti limb sprawl
smart cocktail bar tea dance misplaced gentility
Moscow Mule, premixed horse kick.

Queue for the toilets
camouflage trousers Greek fisherman's cap
eyed one another nameless
no discussion, into stall together
crowded up clothes rucked
rustling line outside *shh*
bursting behind cubicle door
found her inside seam cleave cleft
arrowed to the line splitting the middle
breathed *More*

Really? I slipped second hand into cup of the first.
Held them both there, she all a-quiver,
my every move a telegraphed message,
nestled palms bone-cradled there:
hot sheath, glowing altar, another new world.

Her felt moan: *O*

Coaxed self back from the infinite.
Slipped out *Goodbye*
Thank you

No name or phone number, no contact,
only perfect memory, thrill
of anonymity, my project proceeding apace,
the chance

to focus no distractions
unknown woman's body (learn mine)
open to me never again maybe
strange country couldn't they
see stretch out take it
pure knowledge

seize the

Bitter(s)

* * *

(Oxford Bedsit and London Toilet, Michaelmas 1994)

> *Hang on a minute, one more*
> *time, you've never wanted*
> white shoulders illuminated
> shift in bed sun through window

> *Yeah, well, um, that's*
> take another sip

> *Bear with me. Let me just:*
> *So you think we can*

> *I don't, um, I mean*

and did I? You want to
and you went to
and you met
and you still

Yeah, I, you know

I don't think so, I mean
we talked about it,
didn't we,
I know I
agreed but I

Wide eyes in mirror shocked shocked
narrow recognition
bitter comprehension flutter shut.
Randy. *Hi,* I manage
Fancy seeing you here

Yeah wrings her hands
Maybe for you, innit, but this
kind of thing's just not on see,
thought you were only seeing someone in Oxford.
What's all this then

getting off in the toilets
with some slapper.

Close my empty mouth.
Noble calling and quest,
pure knowledge: crowded stall pushed inside hot catch
doomed to misunderstanding.
Slip the lock, slip out, evade the lineup's
interested collective gaze. Uneducated

can't
possibly understand

Philosophical

* * *

(The Master and Pupil, London, Winter 1994)

You can't possibly understand.
The Canadian ringing felted surface, expanse of green,
scattered miniature globes.
We circled the table.
*People like you think
there's something wrong with us,
just because we want to feel everything.*

Her back curved over
the table. Her face turned up,
white dish. *Not this again.*
Sacred beatings, getting cut, seeing God—
Broke, scattered, straightened. Rolled her eyes.
Please. Spare me.

Continued *I have to drag out my own body by the teeth*
ground the square of chalk
tip into hollow my cue.

Let's see. Rested on her stick.
The courier on the dole, then
the one without a name.
How's your actual girlfriend by the way
or is she still?
Thwack. Sent the first ball into the pocket.
And what about your
mother's visit, haven't
heard a word

Look the Canadian strolled around the table
Bent *crack* number five orange rolled quietly over the edge:
The rest of us, those you so quaintly consign
to progress's backside
irrelevant passed-over obsolete
Another *thwack.* Number three dropped.
Wouldn't be getting a shot in edgewise
this game

Well guess what, we do
have our virtues, we
don't fuck around, and also
if we do we certainly don't get discovered
doing it in a toilet stall
of all places, and also if we do
two balls left on the table
we're ashamed instead of proud.

And also bent sighted aimed
haven't heard a word about your supervisor.

So what about this degree, what about your real *work,*
why you're supposedly actually here at the

end of the day they're paying you
sunk the eight ball
to study, aren't they,
and I don't think this is what they

had in mind when

Season(al)

* * *

(Oxford and Paris, Christmas 1994)

Long vac, time to decamp
college rented out the rooms
to visiting Americans, Oxford experience,
two thousand quid a fortnight,
no contest.

So if you wouldn't mind
(domestic bursar's fluting tones on the telephone)
Thank you very much indeed

Could have
sunk into ginger ex-girlfriend's
homely flat if not for vague sense of
the Canadian's prediction—true, it turns out—
Haven't seen Randy
since our sink-front meeting, Pearl's mouth in a
thin line turned away
from me now at the bar,
bit disastrous overall,

lesson learned too late if at all.

Proceeding excellently. Good work.
Happy Christmas, standing, Moral Tutor's
limp hand shaking mine.
My stuttered *Oh, um, you too.*

French girl across the landing
not going home herself,
nonetheless brokers
an introduction
to her parents.

(Christmas orphan,
lovers' relatives no solution,
everyone quarrelling, drunk, or glum.
Alone no better.)

Awkward visit
ask for raw endive
they look on politely aghast
Parisian horror
at the mismanagement
of lettuce.

Christmas Day.
Half bottle too-sweet Sauternes,
shut shops. Dull coins, pocket scrabble, cobble a meal
from train station vending machine:
Plops brand peanut puffs,
empty hostel room.

Hard Bar

* * *

(The London Apprentice, Shoreditch, 1995)

Saving my
embarrassment
the congregants ignored
my shifting sideways glances
took in their
nightly communion,
featherweight boxes of crisps,
chicken and chili
I'll go—second floor
darkroom translucent panels stopped short

floorboards ankles feet occasional
elbows puzzle pieces clues to
all the shrouded
rest, shadowed
machine-like: pistons, oil derricks,
calves bulging knelt
to receive—

Arrowed the length of the room
to rest burning cheeks
against glass,
sign swinging below,
shirtless boy
rubbed off—

Ache in the throat *Men have it all*
Then the arrival of my American counterpart like an answer*

Said you worked here
wanted to check it out
Meet my friend from San Francisco

Friend shook hand *Hi*
lazy grey eyes
eyebrow barbell (Chip, 1994–95)
Yes I didn't say
beefy forearms rolled plaid sleeves
spotlit in dark booth nursing one
de-alcoholized bottle
work break finally
arrived at table palms

*From Oxford, same scholarship.
Same claim to fame. First one to come out and win
in her country as in mine.

loosened sudden sweat thigh rub surreptitious
I'm ready descending
to the underworld, stomach
knotted with pleasure
barbell shouldering
men before us Red Sea
empty bathroom stall click shut out
Chip braced herself arms spread fingers gripping top edge
I pressed in, both of us
yielding flesh against cheap knocked-together partitions
crowded up, clothes rucked, bursting behind cubicle door.
Our breath her *Yes* my urgent discovery.
Another new world inside.

Afterwards whispered in my still-burning ear
someone outside
stroked my hand
the whole time.
Only then did I remember
half-opaque glances
never once surprised

Tender Bitten

* * *

(London Apartment, Spring 1995)

Saving my hostess
embarrassment

I ignore her
writhing on the floor underfoot
raise my feet slightly
as when somebody comes by with the vacuum.
Another warm sip
of middling red, voice rising
over her moans
Oh, is that really where you get
the best leatherwork?
Fingering blackened collar spike
short of breath (again)
buckled almost too tight.

Strapped in strapped down snapping stiff
cuffs close. Skin's give, suck and slip, under
rubber sweat gather. Dressed the part, sure, but why
do none of us join the hostess on the floor?
Every woman here (patting down
floor-length PVC gown, tight
gleaming barrel, chemical pelt
licked almost clean smears
all but invisible) for an orgy and only she
(rolling now—spiky-haired
boyish type, *quite fanciable,* I try)
exposes herself cries
despair and triumph
disbelieving til the last
sprawled limbs and all.
I sit frozen like everyone else
next to the German with the accent
and studded band round her throat.
Guttural spit: Couldn't
even.

We all do though.
Someone else
to take charge
reach out a fleshy hand.
Here.
Recall us: owned
permission
(Forcing a way now)
gasp *No, no, no, cry out Yes, yes, yes,*
bridle tossed head
go down
to dusk-drowning parks
(following the men, curse their anatomical advantage)
in my harnessed condition
fit in, blunt fact, silicon peel
slick scentless slipped out new-born

sink to our knees
in sheer-hung silent rooms
cubicled chambers otherwise empty
stretch out our arms *take*
eat
this body

sound of
bathroom stall doors
slamming ricochet

Break/Try Again

* * *

(London, Spring 1995)

Look, I have to tell the truth, this is hard, but: you're boring.

> *That's it?*

We're just, you know,
it was fun, in the bathroom downstairs at the bar, and
when you took me to the park with all those guys, we saw, and then
>   *we—*
well, you know.

> *You're looking for someone*
> *to take charge.*
> *Give me another chance.*

No, I

One more time. Then if you still want to break up, fine.
Tomorrow night, okay?
Just be ready.

Sat on the sill. A hot night,
window open. Squeal of tires, getaway car.
Seen from above, foreshortened bodies,
car interior lit by dome, pale limbs under glass, metal struts.
Chip's close crop, combat fatigues, stormed up the walk,
face turned to mine from below,
snarl:

> *I said be ready.*
> *What the hell is this?*

I am ready. Martini glass, overfull, on the ledge.
Could have spilt. Hatched bodysuit,
struggled breasts, guppies netted under.

> *For the love of—Put this on.*
> Back of the neck, shaken kitten, tie off,
> blinded now, into the car. Took off.

Dust in my nostrils as the car bucked over humped
zebra crossings. Stifled laughter above. Bump into legs drawn
    back.

Out of the car,
cheerful invisible goodbyes, cracked walk,
blindfold's edge, triangle of sight:
house, room, doorway.* Shackled. Spreadeagle.
Chip's voice, as I swayed stripped. *How do you want it.*

Listen...

Hit me for the first time.
Call me Sir. Count.

Breath knocked. Dragged in air.
Yes, Sir.

One. And then more. Thudding blows.
Peace finally
my body taken located understood explained.
Then the clips, biting. I twisted.
A little less of that, my lady,
Chip said.

Sorry, muttered.

*Belonged to a
famous lesbian photographer
knew her only slightly, lent for the occasion
turned out
abduct someone
(friends' car)
blindfold none too securely, turned out
take to a
previously unknown location
play murder ballads
on the stereo
CD on repeat
all night

She loosed the clamps.

Cried almost. The blood gushed back,
I floated. Such relief.
Finished? No. Of course not.
That would be too easy, too little punishment
for all I've done, and not.

Omnipotent all-seeing. She held up the tubing,
the bulb. Guided me. The stink rose. Shit.
Fill and empty. Rotten inside,
no matter how many times sluiced.
No surprise.
I'd always known.

Oblivion.
Me no more.

Old World

* * *

Thick-walled computer room,
cavern curve, ever-present mechanical humming.
Faint whiff from rowers' practice room next door.
Blinking block cursor, beige plastic keyboard,
motionless heads, black screens, messages from other worlds.

Mick's email: *Continued your researches?*
As in what we did? Don't think I've forgotten,
I've never forgotten you, if only—

Anyway. Tell me more.
Not about them, sounds like you're pretty popular over there,
hah, lots of experience, can I guess?
Have I ever really studied my hands before?
This crouching ceiling?
The grave supplicants' faces?
I look away.

Do I guess right?
Anyway hope to hear
wish you would
like to know
what you're
you know

Meet the President

* * *

(Oxford, Trinity Term 1995)

The college had a
vested interest.
Honorary degree.
Favoured son's pilgrimage.
Members' book spread at his name.
Master's hand
pressing the spot.

Same teeny flagged court
lined up, Singaporean
student across from me unfurled
a lettered banner
windowsill, college
officials buzzing,
nervous as bees.
Can't do anything.
My fellows fresh
hair and outfits polished
new rub.
Ceremonial procession. A clasp each.
Found him opposite.
Slid my fingers against his fleshy mount.
Slowly
wrung his.

Wardrobe Consultation

* * *

(Oxford, Trinity Term 1995)

So what are you wearing?
Their perennial petition:
topless to a
going down or coming up dinner.

Please. Wrong
occasion, I snort. *Manners.*
Choose a T-shirt knotted tight.
Scrawled depiction of a Homicidal Lesbian Terrorist,
barrel of gun pointed at the viewer: *Call 1-800-Blow-U-Away*

You're wearing that?
Sure why not. Not my President.
Astonishment at their sudden sleekness
when they reappear
understand now. Each meeting so much to everyone.
A story to tell, in their glorious futures. *Oh yes. The time I.*
Will I be an exception? Remain silent? No. Not exactly.
Stand in the court below my window.
No plaque to mark where I clasped Ginger, narrow single bed.
So long ago, so many
bodies since, so much learned.
Here come the man and his wife in the flesh
hot sun beating down for once
on our heads bent as for royalty graced.
Stops. Extends a hand. No eyelash flicker
that he's read my shirt's message
though behind him the large men in suits stiffen—

Mr. President I murmur *Please*
Reconsider your stance
Don't Ask Don't Tell
His weary hand in mine.

Body

* * *

(Oxford, Trinity Term 1995)

How I'd sat and spun
night after night, desperate to save—
my voice
extolling the text. *Sex,*
for these female characters—

Um-hm. The Moral Tutor bent under the weight
of books pressing in all around.
A pulse in his throat where I thrummed too—

But what about Freud?
How do you take his notion
of the Unheimlich?
Have you compared translations?
Are you reading the Hogarth edition?

Sure. Trundled again to the Camera, whitewash
under the dome. Submitted: *search me.*
Clear plastic sheathed
Lillets slipped through a
reddened hand. Another porter's thick fingers.
Price of admission, great Scholarship, precious volumes.
Apply at the desk. In case of
fainting couch
in the anteroom of the Ladies'
on the landing. Nodded straight-necked, thrust
my reticule—*snap*—nestling
in my moistened palm, little slip and slide,
recaptured, precious.

Official letter, smoothed white paper, read again.
What does it mean?

Failed to qualify.

Just a formality he assured
nothing to worry about. A few—

tap tap. Lined.

So I
bent again to the task,
imprisoned as the miller's
beautiful daughter in a roomful of straw.
Undergraduates hooting in the lane Saturday night,
leaving spattered vomit circles
for Sunday morning. Same official
letterhead, return address, same words again.
What do they mean?

I told you, Tutor's blue-eyed gaze.

Had performed
maidenly duty
shining piles all around,
hadn't I?

I told you
it would never pass

Blow

* * *

(Shoreditch, London, Summer 1995)

Maidens in toilets,
closets, rooms overhead.
Gold coins dropped
dark gutter.

How I kneel and pray
lucky, glimmering nights
murmured *Yeses* in the dark.
Our silent watching chorus—
witnesses, such devotion, touching
really, if I say so
myself.

Vault a fence, over easy, locked gate
no obstacle to our seeking. Get inside.
Settled flesh, cold concrete plinth
But what about you?

Yes
parted skirts, liquid gasp
bare thighs scraping against her Levi's,
hot well
cored.

Footsteps on the path
outside the cemetery
clicking away breath *Stop*

man on a bicycle
faraway path bisecting ours,
straight ahead stare, then
out of our sight *Let's go*
tumble back into living world,
vivid sodium street light glow,
pull up, reel on, top deck,
late-night drunk bus
leering lads set up a hue
Go on then, what are you like

Safe enough squeezed gush secret looks
between us we remember my pleadings.
Punish me for everything I've forgotten
that should have been a permanent memory:
strange lips, folded, lavish,
rising ripe.

Round the circle thigh to thigh,
lurch and swivel her weight press
hoots from behind, rested shoulder,
hand in hers, my breath landing
between collarbone and ear,
tender nestle, grateful to be shown (again).
Greed stilled, yawning
cavity brimming.
Just like
every other time.

Laying down of the lash,
striped cane scalpel's slice candle drip
gas mask breathing loud in my ears,
sudden prick of little sharp
in the fleshy mount
between finger and thumb,
sudden spike of pleased surprise *Ah*

Home waits patient as ever. Separate peace
credit rating wiped clean.
dip body into sea, let hot sun for once
burn away sins.
Vanished,
scot-free, just as I'd
planned and wanted and decided I deserved.
Old country, new world for my plunder.
So maybe I don't have to spin the straw as I imagined.
Maybe the door never locked,
swung open at a touch.

Marks heal, burns fade.
No guarantee no body ever promised.
Only these particular nights
and each other.

Selfless.

Bloody

* * *

(Vauxhall Tavern, London, Summer 1995)

You could stop with me for a bit

I suppose but won't that
be a bit of an inconvenience
your girlfriend and all

Hardly Canadian's council flat being done up.
Sex show south of the river
I'll drive you

Front of the pub underneath the overpass.
Sat with my fellows. Stage lights dimmed. One spot.

The top arrived onstage first, swaggering.
Leather jodhpurs, uniform jacket buttons' dull gleam,
shining cap, glossy visor, hooded eyes.
Creak of our like leathers leaning closer.

The girl next, predetermined victim.
Thrust from backstage, looked,
stumbled to master's side, lost.
Thick blond dreads
and a slip dress.
Crescendo of soundtrack,
crashing chords.
Snipped slip puddled
at her feet
slight white body beneath.
Turned, traced, beaten (back),
taken and pressed trouser seam
and creased fly,
stretched moment, trembled and thrust,

still on her knees.
Angry buzz of metal.
First of her locks fell.
Our whisper rose again, frowns, *too much*
pictures huddled naked bodies *never again.*
Still only a murmured mutter,
we watched as the top clipped away.
The girl's head shone bare.
Oh we must have imagined smiled our relief
She bent, swayed,
chain swung out,
caught the light flickered gaze *No*
Star of David hanging there.
Silence.

Show

* * *

(Vauxhall Tavern, London, Summer 1995)

Thought I'd come get you
just pulled up
glad I did

what happened
what's wrong
how are

just drive fell into the seat
Canadian steered, patted me
without looking *what is it tell me*
did somebody hurt you

I started to laugh
the absurdity of it, my refuge and blind
violate now
replayed the show:
top's uniform,
naked slave, head shorn

Canadian interrupted *But why?*
The slave I mean.
Who agrees to that?

That's not all I haven't told you
six-pointed star pendant
caught in the light

But that's horrible disgusting why it's practically

I know—

Why didn't anybody say anything,
why didn't any of you stop it, you just sat there watching.

I don't know we thought at first we'd imagined
*the uniform—*Coincidence *we said.*
Of course it seemed similar once she'd stripped the girl.
Didn't know for sure
until she shaved her head,
until we saw the star
And by then—

just sitting there watching,
anyway we thought
It'll be over soon.

Button Fly

$* \quad * \quad *$

(Vauxhall Tavern, London, Summer 1995)

Sex show
procurer's sudden appearance,*

*One other time tried to pick me up
at the conference where I met Pearl
wanted one more
for their foursome

Pearl
ascended the stairs all caped glory
bald head tilted up
eyes met

Her? Recognized our
mutual inability, take charge, come over.
No need no word.
Smiled through

all-knowing waiter,
message for me: *Come.*
House uniform, spotless white T, bound breasts,
501s, broad leather belt, brass buckle
closed button fly brush cut
uniform look
Expression purely neutral.
A simple job, I imagined; fetch someone,
mistresses' imperious order: *Find.*
I rose as if waiting until then,
followed her prosaic jean-clad legs' rustle
upstairs past locked doors,
dim forms of humped furniture,
shadows behind glass. The miller's daughter,
willingly, again.

———

absurdity of it, impossibility
we could ever
be naked to each other
like that. *Hilarious* I tried.

Some years had passed though
so I suppose the messenger

didn't recognize me now
even though I hadn't changed I thought
not one bit.

Hold Fast

* * *

(Vauxhall Tavern, London, Summer 1995)

Flickering candle glow casts guttering pool,
spilt light. Draped chairs, pair of strange women,
leather jackets, stamped metal ears, calm serious faces.
Doctors of physiognomy? I kneel as if told,
ease off each item. They examine me in silence. Verdict.
Smell my own excitement and worry will I
rich enough pretty
yielding silent acquiesce
perform *please* shut eyes
give up over
speak as told
or not

Hold me in gloved hand, push,
not yet yielding sheath,
purse clutch tight, reticule click on Freud's couch.
Body's less than immediate give, my inability,
clenched fist push harder.
Always suspected I'd be
found wanting. *Here*, and an amyl vial
broken under my nose,
expand and contract but still can't lose alarm
(strangers) shut protect
batten block timbers iron girded
Welcome (Go Away)

Body's
little aperture first citadel
of memory
not to be
taken again

Story

* * *

(Point Grey, 1981, London, 1995)

I had never quite
believed in my body, its
appearance, the space it took up.
When I was a child my father left*
and a family, strangers, took me in.
So nice, went everybody.
Until my new father
asked me to take
him in.

*For the weekend, he assured—
turned out to be years

Learned what you could do
with an abandoned girl.*
Put his—
(could tell what I really wanted, he said)
hands and mouth on me—

pale thighs held close, two breasts not yet
formed—
beckon
him signs invisible**
rose under
like bread, tossed

*Abandoned myself in turn, didn't I,
  synthesized beat of the new music,
  Aqua Net in a toxic cloud,
  shoplifting with Jennifer
  at Nordstrom's, plastic clip-ons,
  white cardboard box,
  sharp-eyed store detective,
  bleached pale jean capris,
  tight button, Calvin Klein,
  you can have them easy come
  mickey handed over in the
  liquor store
  parking lot—*Thanks, mister.*

Lungful of hashish smoke. Hold.

Why are you doing this
  the social worker
  Again?

**You blame yourself,
  self-preservation: easier to
  condemn self-betrayal than the world
  that let this happen or the man
  so much bigger.

in quiet loathing
snake of
secret *can't ever admit*
turned out I wasn't so impervious,
was I?

then five years flesh silenced.
Had to learn mine
later, keen
bring back, bring back,
oh bring back my bonnie to me.

Lessons learned:

1. Pain sucks me back
into flesh undeniable

2. Stop or start my acquiescence at will,
hurt chosen and controlled

3. Live in this body of mine,
forget until required to remember

4. and
again.

Tell

* * *

(Vancouver, 1981 and 1995–present)

I have always
believed in my body, its
power and weight, its dear curves,
scoop, hollow, and bulge,
fleshed excess
eschewing the mother's
concave example

hand half caress,
proprietary
Here I am.

I have smiled fondly at
every gloppy emanation, mined
gooey productions
between thumb and forefinger
random internal stabs, sudden aches, shifts,
cracks and rumblings weight unseen.
Tried to learn
its internal mutterings,
unarticulated needs.
Even the horny scraped bits.

Delicate horse hoof,
loofah pumice dissolving
crème fingernail scrape
white marks in the dust skin
after they sawed off
the cast
You can hardly tell, said the satisfied surgeon.
Skin detritus no visible difference but
marked
at a touch.

Forgiven.

It turns out others aren't so indulgent, are they?
So I chip
the deodorant out of the pot, don't I,
and apply it with a liberal hand
despite its demonstrated failures.
Naturally Effective, humph—
so I decently drape the furry bits,
legs, armpits, taking special care
to do so in what
are described as
professional situations,

loose pants worn almost sheer bulging now,
what when they fail me,
when the warp gives
where to turn at the last?

Oh, it's not much, I say
when others admire my hours
in the bicycle saddle. Unconcealed pride:
tireless circulation, blood red and blue, arteries vague
carp slide under
milky expanse inner arm
nurse's exclamation—*Ooh! Good veins!*

My heart despite my every
steadfast refusal
continuing to beat

Live in this
body of mine:
can never ignore for
one moment

Good Fight/Give It Up

* * *

(London Apprentice, Shoreditch, 1995)

The Canadian flung open
black-painted flimsy.
Sun shot from behind then swung shut out.
OK Corral swagger.
Stood and waited.
So this is where you've been hiding.
What do you think you're doing.
No business giving up like this. Buck up.

      I seized the rag. Began to wipe
      the immaculate bar top. In between swipes:
      No business telling me what to do.
      You don't and never could understand them like I do.

You won that scholarship, didn't you?
Got in, didn't you? You're writing—something about women and
    knowledge? Something brainy. You'd really throw it away?
You can't just leave it like this.
You can't just let them win.
I thought you were a fighter.

> *I am a fighter,* I said, *I am, and fighters*
> *know when fights can't be won.*

Reminded me (as if I needed)
I had one last chance. I'd told her so myself,
hadn't I?

> *There's no*

Are you really just going to walk away from everything?

> *point,* I said.

> *Let me tell you something. I got a letter and it boils down to*
>   *this:*
> *You're done. Meaning me. Only a fool doesn't*
> *get it. They don't want me.*
> *Yes,* I said, *I am going to walk away. Just like that.*
> I felt myself surge, electric. This the answer. Leave myself,
>   leave
> them, even though
> they'd neither notice nor care.

How about a drink then, at least—

I hastened to obey.
She crossed my palm.
The coins' gleam, buffed dull, nestled a moment,
creased hollow
basket of sallow sheathed bone then dropped
—*clang*—into the till. Dispensed a small gin: bitters.
    Lifted my own.
Cheers. First sip. Smiled with relief.
She'd been served.

Funny, she said.
Would have thought you'd learned
by now

Lash Line

* * *

(Brixton, 1995)

All change muffled announcement
we step out then sudden feet
sweep from gritty platform pavement.
Chip's broad forearm
against my thorax,
shutter blink aperture narrowing, black crowd disappears,
tight black hole, man's voice
Everything all—?

Fine, thanks, sir, just helping her up.

Sweet air flooding in stagger
into carriage, Chip's voice
I hate it here what's wrong with everyone,

where's the good coffee they have no good coffee
just fuckin' tea
there's nothing to eat
for fuck's sake

but you swallow find my
there's always shudder stop she shoulders broad back follow
Here
pub windows wavy leaded, cozy
gathered wooden chairs, round tables,
incongruous sunlight pouring down,
bleached coifs, shaved heads,
leather jackets, red lipstick, pale turquoise tutu puff.
You all right? Sure.
Nudge, look down,
strange man on all fours
almost naked leather shorts
whip in his mouth.
You want it?
Take the handle of the crop.
Spell my city's name.

Hit him. Again.

I'd learned. Force in,
bully with fingers and shoulder,
striated roll of muscle,
tense and release.
But what about me?
Eyes roll back,
breathe the word *Yes?*
Slack at the knees? Buckle under? Clutch *Take me?*
My hands, fated (later) to peel back the urine-sodden cloth,
O joy lift small bodies, arms held high, pipes beckon *up up up;*
my flesh, seamed still, squint short sight
amidst juvenile howl, vortex, maelstrom
struck—

The scar I begged Chip—
give me—permanent mark of favour indelible act
Was that?
Did we?
Really
scalpel's clean cut
barely noticeable now
skimming slash, red well closed over
fade to silvery track underneath
one eye

Yesterday

* * *

(London, 1995, and Oxford, 2003 and 2009)

The sky
a sheet of grey, flat, texture pressed from each cloud.
College buildings, built of special stone, quarried
    specifically erected
at fabulous cost, hefty endowment, rock of ages,
midst of island gloom.

Up in London (or was it down?)
we howled on the street, took back
nights, copied our brethren:
pretended avengers.
Our lesbian grottoes admittedly little
visible effect but we went
At least we're doing something.

Straight to the source, arrowed to stone fronts,
impervious, lovers' muse:
You got your degree here? This
is amazing. Besotted:
stone joins overhead, delicate tracery,
cherub-faced tot
roaming the flags. Smocked
yellow dress. Charity shop special.
There you go, luv.
Same turtle-backed
sun under glass
porter's lodge. Same clotted tones,
thick dismissal. *Yes?* Same
smudged sun, fat licked finger,
flutter of falling newsprint revealing another
flat smile from sports page,

two breasts shocked shocked by our gaze
Caught unawares, again. *Whoops. Just happened to—*
Posed with a tennis racket. Balls in hand. *Forgot a shirt.*

No mention
of the courtyard
cries drifting up my defence
in suspense unpredictable outcome.

What happened? someone said
as if I'd spoken
Then I got that set of letters
that apparently
mattered so much to me.

Today

* * *

(Vancouver, 2019)

The sky flat,
a sheet of grey, texture pressed from each cloud.
Soaked stucco, builders' rush
to erect the cheapest, California-style,
razed temperate rainforest.

This my city from infant days—
Remember when?—took blood
without authorization, bared breasts
astride, short in the saddle, traffic cop stop
Calling this one in, ma'am
passing cars slowing to a hot crawl
red tail lights.

(Tell them
how it was.)
On stroller trips men nod
slumped in doorways
(*Amazing*, they repeat)
charge myself
(above infant shrieks)
to kneel and shake them.

You okay?
Free kit
marked grey cross,
anyone's for the asking,
hasty afternoon's training,
ready loaded administer,
reversing other drugs'
unpredictable effects:
overdose,
heart failure,
cardiac arrest.
The slide. Oblivion.
Coroner's report.

Can I save anyone,
least of all
myself?
Open question

Acknowledgements

I HAVE BEEN SHACKLED to this book for quite some time. The knots loosened fractionally when it struck me this was no memoir (too boring), nor a novel (insufficient plot). Rather than confess myself beaten, I continued knocking around the concept, emerging from my writing dungeon finally with a bruisingly complex set of poems running either side of the page (impractical). Splayed across these paper sheets is my final effort. Reader, I beg you: have mercy. I confess I have not mastered the form.

Throughout this process, I have been immensely grateful for the stalwart assistance and wise counsel of my writing partner Maureen Medved. Maureen's insight into what I wanted to say, as well as her focus on how to best serve the reader, helped me articulate precisely what I needed to express, and how. This book is immeasurably better due to her careful attentions.

Sorely needed instruction and correction were kindly provided by Heidi Greco, who urged me to "blow up" the manuscript, Daniel Gawthrop, Brett Josef Grubisic, and John Harris. The latter three experienced the blow-by-blow evolution of this book by proxy. Their faithful service as readers has earned my undying gratitude.

Finally, my thanks to Sand Northrup, my first lay reader and a source of great inspiration in so many forms, who spurred me to reimagine the manuscript in a whole new way. Poetry! Sweet release.

Book*hug itself considered my submissions. All of them. (Thank goodness they said yes in the end.) They even arranged a hard-hitting editor, Jennifer LoveGrove, to lend a firm hand on matters of tense, italics, and footnotes.

Finally, I would like to thank my children for not reading this.

About the Author

Carellin Brooks is the author of *One Hundred Days of Rain*, which won the 2016 ReLit Award for Fiction and the 2016 Edmund White Award for Debut LGBT+ Fiction, and was published in French by Les Allusifs. She is also the author of *Fresh Hell*, *Every Inch a Woman*, and *Wreck Beach*. Brooks lives in Vancouver and is a lecturer at the University of British Columbia.

Colophon

Manufactured as the first edition of
Learned
in the fall of 2022 by Book*hug Press

Edited for the press by Jennifer LoveGrove
Copy-edited by Stuart Ross
Proofread by Charlene Chow

Design, typesetting, and cover illustration by Gareth Lind,
Lind Design, with source stock illustrations by
iStock/PPrat (Oxford skyline), iStock/Kasya 2k (sex toys),
and iStock/Veronika Oliinyk (faces)
Type: Garamond Premier Pro, Berthold Akzidenz,
and Breite Kanzlei

Printed in Canada

bookhugpress.ca